THE MONARCH BUTTERFLY

Miraculous stages and changes

Written and Photographed
by MONICA TAYLOR

SUMMARY:

Two books in one!

After five years of observation, documentation, and photography, it was a privilege to preserve these fleeting moments in time. With over ninety close-up and beautifully detailed photographic images, you will learn about the amazing transformation of the monarch butterfly and the elusive, nocturnal cecropia moth. This book features a spectacular photographic depiction of both the monarch butterfly and the cecropia moth through their entire life cycle. Every step by step image is detailed and explained with clear, kid-friendly language that can also be enjoyed by adults. All the documentation and photography is taken from southern Ontario, Canada.

Monarch butterflies are insects. They live everywhere except in the hottest and coldest places on earth. They weigh less than a five dollar bill. Every year they migrate from southern Canada and the United States up to 4,023 kilometres (2,500 miles) to Mexico. Butterflies west of the Rocky Mountains fly to the coast of California. No other butterfly travels that far! Here is their incredible life journey.

The monarch has four phases in its life:

THE EGG

THE LARVA OR CATERPILLAR

THE PUPA OR CHRYSALIS

THE ADULT BUTTERFLY

There are female and male monarch butterflies. The male monarch has two spots on his lower wings. They are scent pouches that contain pheromones, which is a chemical substance that attracts the female. The female does not have any spots. Monarchs must mate to fertilize the eggs, and now the female is ready to lay her eggs.

(Do not confuse the monarch with the imposter viceroy butterfly, which is smaller. Notice the extra vertical line on its hind wing.)

She finds a milkweed plant and usually lays only one egg at a time on the underside of a leaf or branch. The egg is smaller than the size of a pinhead. After she lays her egg she will then fly to another milkweed plant and lay another egg. A female monarch can lay up to 250 eggs per day, depending on the weather. Monarchs lay fewer eggs in hot, dry summers. On average, they lay about 400 eggs. Only about one in one hundred live to become an adult butterfly, because they are prey, or food, to birds and other creatures and insects. Milkweed is the only plant the monarch larva will eat. It contains toxins that help keep most birds, insects, and other animals from eating them. They are called predators.

The toxins are stored in the exoskeleton of the monarch so that the organs of the monarch don't get too toxic. The exoskeleton is the skin-like soft shell that covers the body. When the larva eats milkweed for the first time, it eats between the veins so that it does not ingest too much right away. When it gets older, the larva will cut off the flow of sap from the vein so that it doesn't take in too much toxin.

In three to six days, the larva will be ready to hatch, or emerge. It will eat its way out of the egg casing.

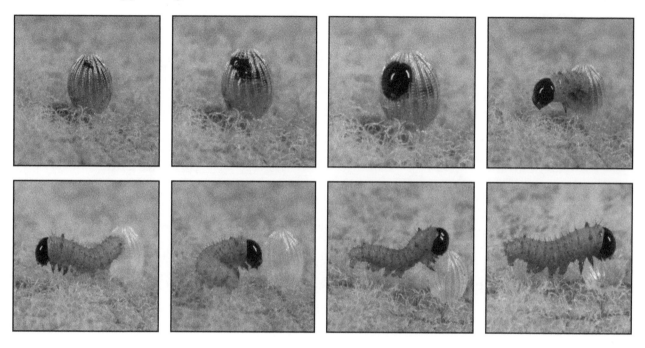

Once it is all the way out, it will turn around and have its first meal—the egg casing.

When it has finished its meal, it will crawl away. First it will eat the small hairs of the milkweed leaf, then the milkweed leaf itself.

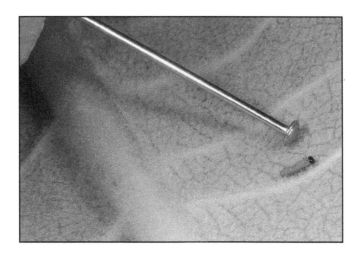

The larva, or first instar, is so small it can barely be seen. It is the size of the head of a sewing pin.

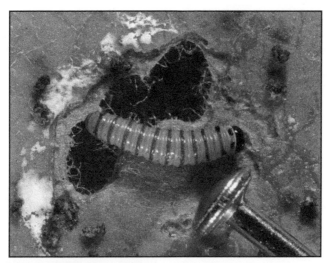

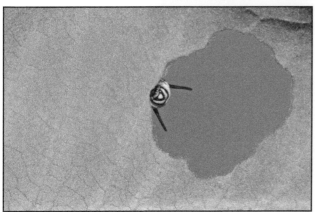
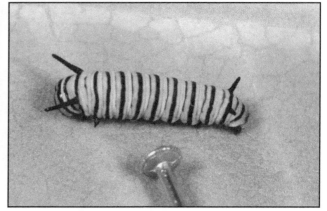

The caterpillar also has strong jaws for chewing leaves. It will eat nothing but the milkweed plant. Because it spends all its time eating, it will grow very quickly. In the fourth and fifth instar, when caterpillars are big enough, they can eat an entire milkweed leaf in less than five minutes! Here's an interesting fact—their jaws do not move up and down like ours; instead, they move sideways.

Within two days, the larva, or caterpillar, will grow almost two times its size. The skin will become so tight it will need new skin. Now it will molt, or shed, its old skin. The skin will split open, and the caterpillar will crawl out of the old skin. The new skin will harden, and the caterpillar will begin to eat again. The first meal is usually the skin they just shed.

Since it is the only plant that they eat, they continue eating the milkweed leaves. Getting bigger and bigger, the skin will once again become too tight, and the caterpillar will have to molt again. This will happen five times in its lifetime. During its ten to fourteen days as a caterpillar, it gains 2,700 times its original weight. If we could grow that fast, a six pound baby would end up weighing about eight tons—about the weight of a school bus!

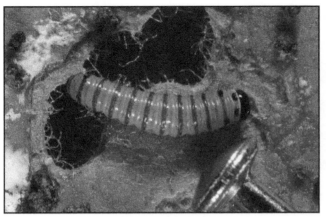

First Instar

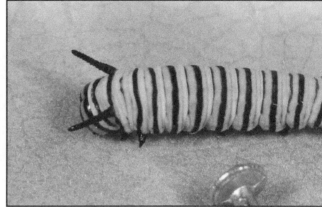

Second Instar

Third Instar

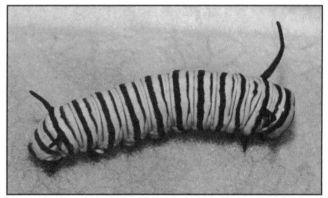

Fourth Instar

These new caterpillars are called first instar, second instar, third instar, fourth instar, and fifth instar. Notice the difference in the legs, antenna, and stripes.

Fifth instar

In nine to fourteen days, it will be about five centimetres long. About the size of your pinky finger, it is now full grown.

The caterpillar's long body has sixteen legs that have hook-like claws. This helps the caterpillar crawl and hold on to the plants. The front six legs will actually become the legs of the butterfly, while the other legs help it to hold on to the milkweed plants.

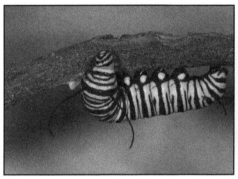 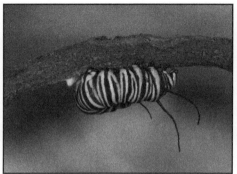 

When it is ready to develop into a pupa, the caterpillar will stop eating for about a day. It becomes very restless as it searches for a place to attach itself, wandering around for hours trying to find that perfect spot on a branch, leaf, or whatever it decides is a safe resting place. When it finds that spot, the monarch larva will spin a silk mat from which it will hang upside down by its back feet. The silk comes from the spinneret on the bottom of the head. As it sheds its skin for the last time, the caterpillar stabs a stem into the silk pad. This stem extends from its rear end and is called the cremaster.

After several hours, it will release its front legs and hang in a "J" shape. It will hang like this for about twenty-four hours.

The next day, the caterpillar is ready to turn into a pupa. First the antenna will become droopy and the body will start to straighten. You will see the skin wriggle in an upward movement. Within seconds, the skin will split by the head and antenna, and the caterpillar will continue to wriggle until the skin compresses and moves up towards the silk pad. Hooks on the cremaster get tangled in the silk pad while the caterpillar is wriggling. This ensures a good hold. Now a miracle happens. Under that skin is the beautiful green chrysalis!

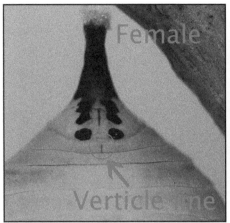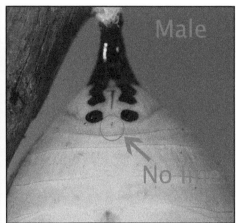

The hard case that covers the pupa is called a chrysalis. Once it hardens, you can determine the sex of the developing butterfly by examining the chrysalis. The female has a small line below the stem.

When the butterfly is ready to come out, the chrysalis will change colour from a jade shade until it becomes clear. Now you can see the new butterfly inside. The process of a caterpillar changing into a butterfly is called metamorphosis. This takes about ten to fourteen days. Now it just has to crawl out and emerge from the chrysalis. The scientific term for this is eclose.

This is the monarch butterfly emerging from the chrysalis. It only takes a few minutes. The butterfly's abdomen is full of fluid, which it will pump into its wings to help them expand, or grow much larger, even after the wings have hardened. Blood flows from the thorax, or body, into the wings and then back into the thorax again. It will rest and dry its wings before it can fly. The wings usually take three to four hours to fully dry.

Now the butterfly is ready to fly. The butterfly uses its eyes to locate flowers, its antenna to smell the nectar, and its feet to taste sweet substances. Adult monarchs feed on nectar and sometimes water from puddles by sipping through a sucking tube called a proboscis. It is coiled under the head when not in use. After feeding, the monarch will find a mate. The scent pouches that release pheromones on the rear wing of the males will attract a female. Soon after mating with the male, the female lays her eggs, and a new cycle of life will begin again.

The last generation is a super generation. These butterflies will not turn into a chrysalis until next year. Their sexual organs will not mature at this time so that they have the energy to migrate. They will fly all the way to Mexico. You may be surprised to learn that it only takes about two months to make this trip. The fall migration advances an average of 40 kilometers a day, stopping to drink nectar and to rest. The nectar is sweet and will provide energy for the long flight. They cannot rest for long, as they are racing against the cold. Even though they have never taken this journey before, their body knows the way.

The monarch's journey is very dangerous, and it often flies as part of a huge group. There is safety in numbers! It may not find enough food, or it may become too tired. It could also get eaten by a bird, insect, or other creatures. The monarch stores poison in its body from the milkweed plant, which makes it taste bitter, but it only keeps some of the predators away, as you can see in the image.

Sometimes bad weather may slow it down or stop it. A monarch cannot fly if its wings get wet or if they get too cold.

Monarchs fly at speeds ranging between nineteen and forty kilometres per hour. They use the updrafts or warm air called "thermals" to their advantage, and they glide to preserve the energy needed for flapping their wings throughout their flight. They will all settle in for the night to get rest and food for their long journey.

From Ontario, they will fly to the oyamel fir trees in the Michoacán Hills in Central Mexico. Scientists know this because every year, thousands of people tag monarchs in Ontario and in the United States before the butterflies migrate. The tag states the monarch's sex and where it was tagged. When people find these tagged butterflies, they report the tag numbers to Monarch Watch, where they document when and where the butterflies were found. As of 2003, a tagged male monarch (Danaus plexippus), released by Donald A. Davis (Canada) at Presqu'ile Provincial Park near Brighton, Ontario, Canada, on 10 September 1988, was recaptured on 8 April 1989 in Austin, Texas, USA. It is assumed that this butterfly spent the winter in Mexico as it would not have been able to survive freezing winter temperatures in Texas. Hence, this butterfly travelled at least 4,635 km (2,880 miles) – a distance obtained by measuring a line from the release site to the overwintering sites and back north again to Austin, Texas, USA, making this the World's Longest Butterfly Migration. However, the actual distance travelled could be double this figure.." **Keeper of the Records Guinness World Records Ltd."**

This is an image of a monarch I tagged and released.

Once they arrive in Mexico, they settle onto a tree with millions of other butterflies. Roosting keeps them warm during the cold evenings. They will rest here for the winter, and the trees will protect them from predators and bad weather.

They will drink from puddles once in a while but not eat very much, storing lots of energy until they are ready to fly again.

As the days become longer and warmer, the monarchs' reproductive organs will begin to mature. In late February, they are ready to mate. They do not have milkweed plants in the mountains of Mexico, and since this is the only plant on which the female can lay her eggs, she knows that she must fly north again. When she reaches her first patch of milkweed, she, along with all the millions of other butterflies, lays her eggs. Once her eggs are laid, her journey ends. Her job is done, and she dies. After a few days, the eggs hatch and the hungry caterpillar emerges. Once again it will grow, shed, grow even larger, turn into a chrysalis, emerge as a butterfly, mate, and then the females will lay eggs. This process will happen several times, with each generation flying further north until they reach Canada.

If you are ever lucky enough to see
a monarch butterfly,

think about the difficult journey it
took to get here. How amazing!

WOULD YOU LIKE TO RAISE A MONARCH BUTTERFLY?

Raising a monarch butterfly requires a lot of responsibility and proper care. It is just like having a pet hamster. Remember, they are endangered, so you must be responsible about raising your caterpillar. If you are willing to clean up the "frass," or poop, as well as make sure they have plenty of fresh milkweed every day, then you are ready to take care of your own caterpillar. You will be amazed at what you will see and experience while raising your monarch!

Here is what you will need:

For the search:

Magnifying glass
To help you identify them. Both the egg and larva are found only on a milkweed plant.

The eggs are very small. Look for the unique ridges on the football-shaped single egg. Also look for frass or 'poop' on the leaves to find larger cats. Look for a semi-circular hole on a leaf and carefully lift it and look underneath. You may

find the larva.

Scissors

To carefully cut the leaf from the milkweed plant. Take home an extra leaf for each egg or larva. If you have large caterpillars, you will need several leaves. Wrap the ends in a wet paper towel and store in the fridge.

Fruit and veggie, bakery containers or bug catcher

Use these to safely take the butterflies home, as they are extremely fragile. You can also use them for the first couple of days after they hatch, as they make a great nursery.

Now to raise them:

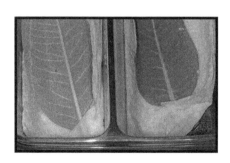

Plastic container lined with towel and corner over stem of milkweed.

If they are first instars or eggs, they should be placed in a plastic container lined with a damp paper towel with a fresh milkweed leaf placed on top. The moisture will help keep the milkweed fresh. Make sure the milkweed was picked from a field or garden that has not been sprayed with insecticides. Always wash the leaves with clean water and towel dry. Keep the lid on tight, as they can crawl out. There is enough air in the sealed container for the larvae.

Bug catcher with pantyhose covering lid.

By the second instar, you can move them to a larger container. When they are too large to fit through the holes in the bug catcher, you can remove the pantyhose. Leave the lid on so that they cannot crawl out.

 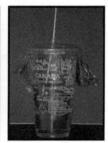

Medium plastic drink cup or a small aquarium

You require a screen lid for when they get larger. You can stand up the milkweed stem and leaves in the plastic drink cup covered with saran wrap under the lid. Just poke a hole in it. The size of aquarium or container depends on how many cats you are raising. Did you know that we call the caterpillars "cats"?

Spray bottle

Use this to keep the paper toweling damp (not wet) in the nursery container and to spray the floral foam (if you use this).

Use lots of paper towels to line the nursery for your caterpillars. Wrap wet ones around the ends of the milkweed leaves to keep them fresh. Important: Make sure there are no monarch eggs or caterpillars on the leaves before you wash them! Just use plain water.

Access to lots and lots of fresh milkweed: They won't need much the first few days, but as they get larger, they become eating machines!

If you have to keep the butterfly for more than a day because of weather, you will need to feed them. They can eat nectar, regular Gatorade, or a piece of fruit like watermelon or orange slices.

Recipe for Nectar: Get an adult to help. Four parts water to one part sugar or honey. Boil the sweet solution until the sugar has dissolved and cool completely. Soak a cotton ball in the solution and place on the bottom of enclosure.

How to Care for Your Cats

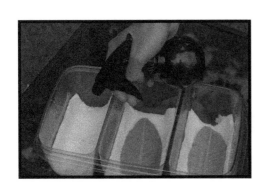

You will need to line your container with a clean, moist paper towel. Place the milkweed end on the paper towel, turning in the corners over stem to ensure the leaf gets water.

If you find eggs, line a small container with a damp paper towel, turning in the corners over stem to ensure the leaf gets water. Place the leaf egg-side up. Cover with a tightly fitting lid. They will hatch in approximately three to six days, depending on the weather or indoor temperature so make sure you continue to spray the toweling to keep it damp, but not wet. You do not want to dehydrate the egg.

Note: If you find a larger cat, place it directly into the aquarium. Do not place the newly hatched larva or eggs with the larger cats, because they might eat them!

During the first week of the newly hatched larva, you need to gently introduce the new leaf. Never touch the larva or you could kill it, as it is very fragile. Gently lift the leaf with the cat on it and slide the new leaf underneath, placing the edge of the new leaf close to the cat so that it can easily crawl onto it. After it has crawled onto the new leaf, remove the old one and compost what is left. No rush. Sometimes they are quite at home on the old leaf and may stay there for days until it is completely withered. Don't worry, as long as the fresh leaf is there the larva will crawl over to get the fresh milkweed when it needs to eat.

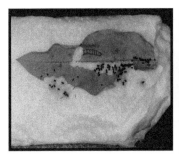 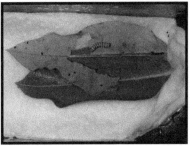

New leaf under old

Caution: If you notice that your cat has not moved for a day or two and still looks healthy, it has not died. It is just preparing to molt or shed. Take extra caution and ***do not move it***. This is a very fragile time for the cat, and it can die if moved during this process.

Sometimes it will just crawl up to the top of the lid and hang upside down for a day. After it molts, it will eat the skin then continue eating the milkweed again.

As mentioned previously, in about ten to fourteen days it will pupate, usually in the early morning, after hanging in a "j" formation all night. Leave the chrysalis alone in the clean container and wait for about two weeks for the butterfly to emerge. The chrysalis will become darker in colour the night before the monarch emerges. If you look carefully, you can actually see the butterfly inside. They usually emerge in the morning. You should wait a couple of hours for the wings to dry after they emerge. Take your container outside to release the butterfly. You can put your finger under their "legs" and they will walk onto your finger. You can either let them stay on your finger and observe them until they are ready to fly, or hold them next to a nectar flower and they will hop onto it. If you put some nectar in your hand or even on your nose, usually they stay for a while! This is a great time to get some beautiful pictures of your monarch butterfly. If it is a rainy or cold day, do not release your butterfly. They cannot fly, so they will make easy prey for a bird or other creature. Make sure you have nectar available for it to sip. You can place a few nectar-soaked cotton balls on the bottom of the aquarium. The butterfly will live comfortably for a day or two until you release it when the weather is dry and, hopefully, sunny. Wasn't it amazing to watch the transformation?

Congratulations! You just made a difference to the population of the monarch butterfly.

Plant a butterfly garden to attract the butterflies.

You need to plant both nectaring flowers as well as host plants to lay eggs on.

Here are a few suggestions:

Host plants for the monarch:

- swamp milkweed
- common milkweed

If you would like to attract some different butterflies in your garden:

Host plant for black swallowtails

- dill, fennel, rue, or Queen Anne's lace

Host plants for giant swallowtails:

- rue or a hop tree

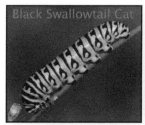

A few great nectaring flowers are:

- marigold
- lantana
- zinnia
- blazing star
- purple coneflower
- oregano
- garlic chives

Do you know the difference between a butterfly and a moth? It is a lot like the difference between a frog and toad. They look the same, but behave very differently.

FUN FACTS ABOUT THE BUTTERFLY AND THE MOTH

Both insects start their lives as hungry caterpillars before turning themselves into flying adults.

Butterflies feed on nectar from flowers and drink liquids such as rain water and the juice from rotting fruit. They taste with their feet.

Some moths do not eat or drink at all, living only on the fat in their bodies until they mate and die.

Most moths are nocturnal. This means they fly and feed at night

Butterflies are diurnal. This means they fly and feed during the day.

If you watch a large-winged, flying insect make its way towards a candle at night, it's probably a moth.

When you see a large-winged insect feeding from a flower in the middle of a spring afternoon, it's probably a butterfly.

The butterfly has antennae that look almost like two pieces of wire with a bulb on the end. They almost look like golf clubs.

Often moths' bodies are plumper and fuzzier than butterflies' bodies.

A moth has feathery antennae. They look almost like combs.

Most butterflies pupate as a naked chrysalis.

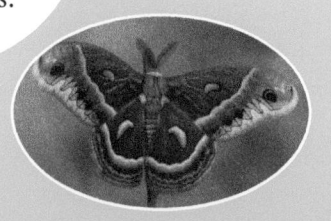

Most moths spin silken cocoons to pupate, sometimes camouflaging it with leaves or debris.

CPSIA information can be obtained
at www.ICGtesting.com
Printed in the USA
LVHW071820261018
594964LV00004BA/11/P

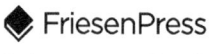 FriesenPress

Suite 300 - 990 Fort St
Victoria, BC, V8V 3K2
Canada

www.friesenpress.com

To contact or order more books, please email mtaylor1529@hotmail.com

ISBN
978-1-5255-1495-1 (Hardcover)
978-1-5255-1496-8 (Paperback)
978-1-5255-1497-5 (eBook)

1. NATURE, ANIMALS, BUTTERFLIES & MOTHS

Distributed to the trade by The Ingram Book Company

THE CECROPIA MOTH

Miraculous stages and changes

Written and Photographed
by MONICA TAYLOR

ABOUT THE AUTHOR:

Monica Taylor is a Canadian photographer from Bowmanville, Ontario. With a love for nature, Monica's dream is to create a sense of wonder and excitement in both the young and old, celebrating this amazing yet fragile world of ours. Explore the beauty and complexity of nature through the art of photography.

I was born and raised in Scarborough, Ontario, Canada. I currently reside in the beautiful historic town of Bowmanville, Ontario. I have always loved nature and the feeling of being grounded every time I had the opportunity to go north.

A late bloomer to the art of photography, I got quite involved in the Oshawa Camera club, winning many awards for my nature images, mainly birds. While looking for birds, I discovered a whole new world! It started with a single monarch caterpillar. I did my research and found out how to raise one. I photographed the many stages as it shed its skin and grew. One day to my surprise it turned into a chrysalis. A number of days later, an amazing monarch butterfly emerged. It was love at first sight. The following year I found the eggs and photographed the entire process. I was so amazed and touched by the process that I wanted to share it with my two grandsons. They have even had the experience of releasing tagged monarchs.

One day while looking for monarch eggs, I came across a cecropia moth. This moth is mostly nocturnal and rarely seen in the day. She was also fertile and started laying eggs. I decided to raise them like I did with the monarch. I knew it would be a privilege to experience the process and that they would have a better chance at survival. They normally have a 10 per cent success rate due to predation, so I took her home. To my surprise, she laid over one hundred eggs, and they started to hatch. I was so excited! I wanted to share the experience, so with detailed instructions on how to care for them, I gave them away to many friends and released a number of them back onto some host plants. I even gave a few to my ninety-year-old father-in-law. He was simply enthralled by the whole process, feeding them daily, cleaning their cage, and watching them turn a different colour each time they shed. He called me daily with a report on their progress. We were all in awe. One day they turned into cocoons, and then we waited. They overwinter here in Canada, unlike the monarch. To our surprise, they all emerged in the spring, and the grandkids released them into nature. After about five years, I decided to give my grandsons a photo book for Christmas so they could preserve their memories. I showed them to some family and friends. They were so amazed by the detail and information that they encouraged me to sell them.

I hope this book will encourage you to stop and notice the tiny things in nature that are a big part of our fragile world. Yours to discover and protect!

- A great resource for primary teachers, camp counselors and children's clubs.
- Two inspirational books in one!
- Written in kid-friendly language.
- Beautifully detailed photographs of both the Monarch butterfly and Cecropia moth at every stage.
- A tactile resource for a child to reference for school projects or an educational hobby.
- A wonderful, informative gift for nature lovers, both young and old.

DEDICATION:

This book is dedicated to Jacob and Spencer, my amazing and inquisitive grandchildren. I hope this book will encourage them to stop and notice the tiny things in nature and make a positive difference in our fragile world.

ACKNOWLEDGEMENT:

I would like to thank my partner, Joanne Carr, for her continual love, support, and encouragement. I also thank her for putting up with my photographic/laboratory studios of jars, containers, and aquariums full of eggs, caterpillars, and chrysalides in our kitchen, living room, and even our trailer while camping!

I would also like to thank Laurel Merriam for reviewing the accuracy of information. Laurel Merriam is a special education resource teacher with Kawartha Pine Ridge District School Board, teacher, and lead facilitator for the Monarch Teacher Network of Canada.

THE LIFE CYCLE OF THE CECROPIA MOTH

The cecropia moth is North America's largest native moth and is from the giant silk moth family. They are not seen very often during the day because they are nocturnal. That means they come out at night. They have a wingspan of five to seven

inches. These moths can be found east of the Rocky Mountains in the United States and southern Canada. The only purpose in the life of the adult moth is to mate and lay eggs. Adult moths cannot eat because they do not have a mouth. If a predator does not scoop them up, they die after two weeks. Cecropia moths have only one generation per year. This is their incredible life journey.

**The cecropia moth has
four phases in its life:**

The egg

The larva, or caterpillar

The pupa, or cocoon

The adult moth

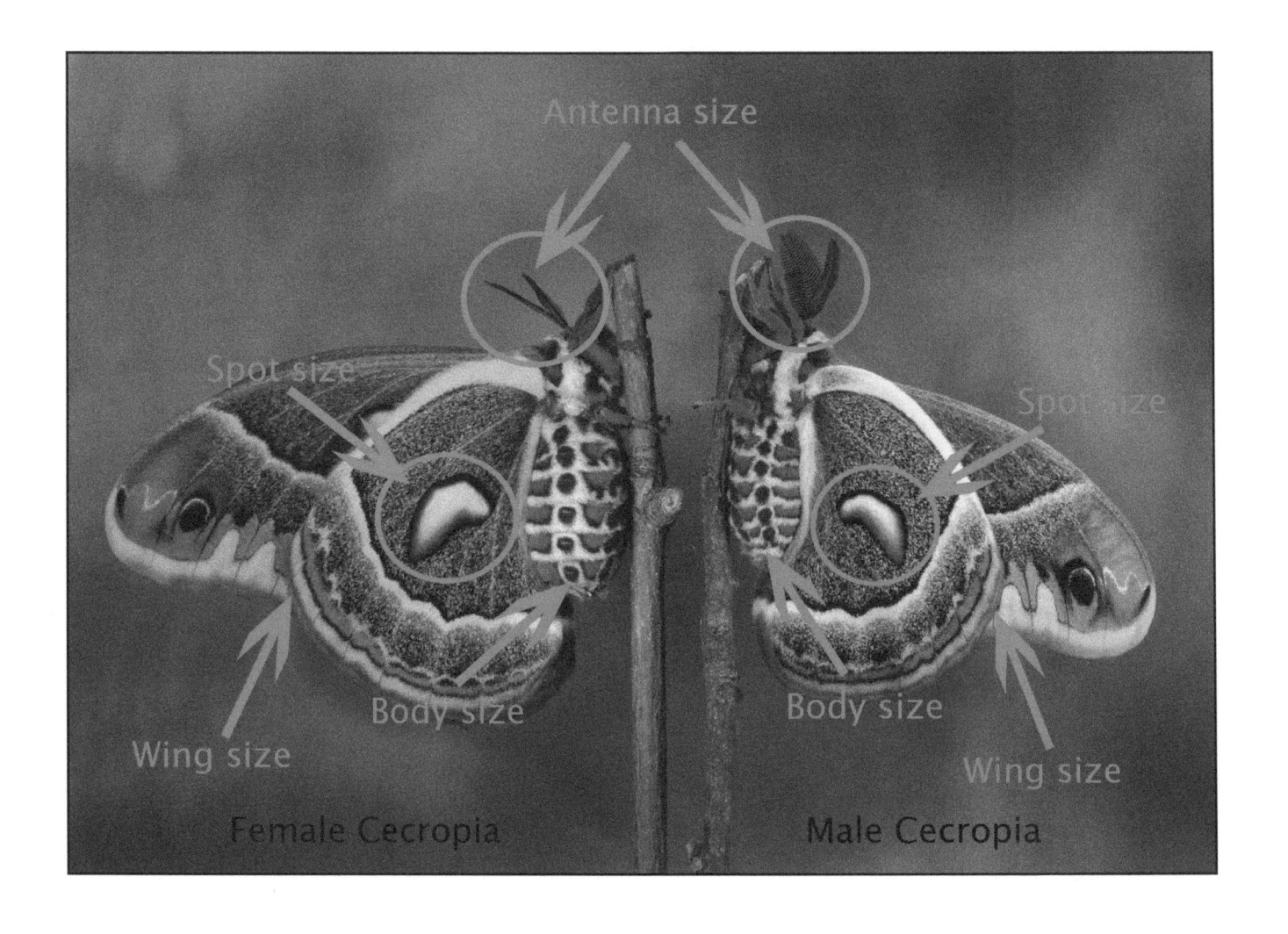

There are female and male cecropia moths. The female cecropia is larger. She has smaller antennae; however, she has a larger abdomen and wings. The spot on her lower wings is also larger. The male is smaller, but he has larger antennae. The abdomen, wing size, and the spot on his wing are all smaller than the female's.

Cecropia moths must mate to fertilize the eggs. Late at night, the female releases chemicals called pheromones. With his large feathery antennae, the male can detect

her pheromones from almost two kilometres away. He can fly up to eleven kilometres while searching for a female. Once he has found a female, the mating begins in the early morning and lasts until the early evening. That's up to twelve hours!

After they mate, the female is ready to lay her eggs. She finds a leaf, tree, or shrub where she can lay her eggs. This will be the host plant for the larvae to eat. Unlike the monarch butterfly, which will only go to the milkweed plant, the cecropia moth goes to a large variety of plants. These include: ash, birch, box elder, alder, elm, maple, poplar, wild cherry, plum, apple, lilac, and willow.

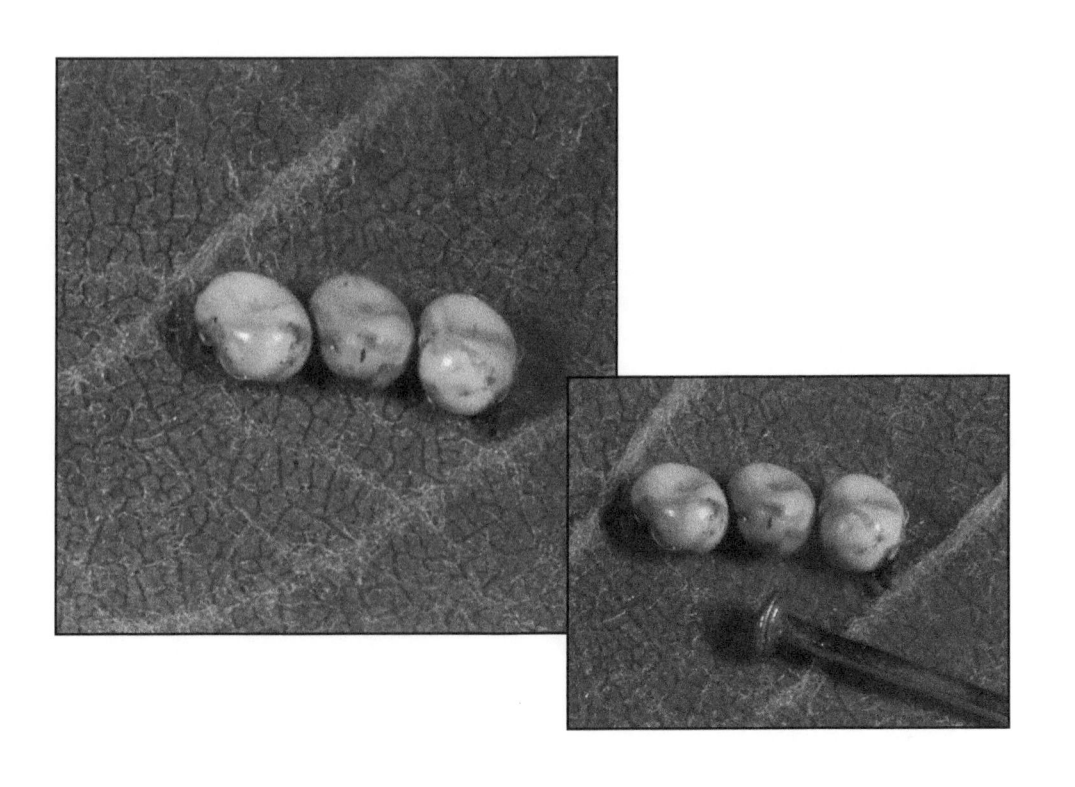

The female lays the eggs in rows of two to six on both sides of the leaves of the host tree or shrub. The eggs are oval-shaped and light brown. They look like they are glazed. This is the glue that the moth uses to stick to the plant. It is not sticky when dry. She lays over one hundred eggs! She needs to lay many eggs, because they are prey, or food, to many insects, birds, and other creatures. Not many survive to become an adult cecropia moth.

 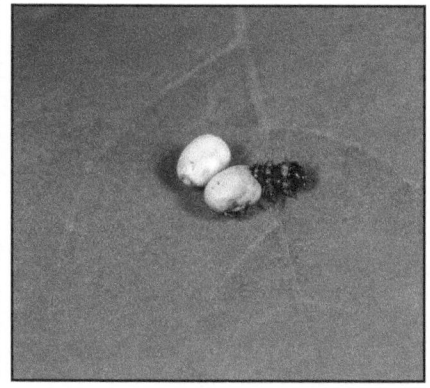 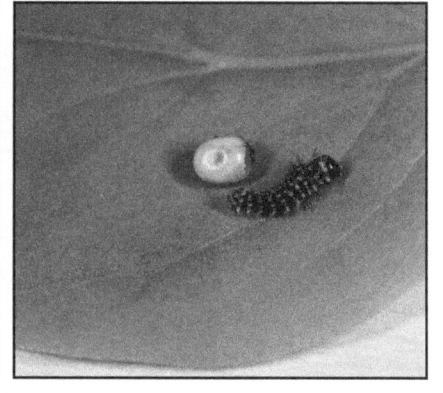

Depending upon the weather, it takes seven to fourteen days for the eggs to hatch. When they are ready to hatch, they will chew a hole in the egg and crawl out. Then they will turn around and have their first meal—the egg casing.

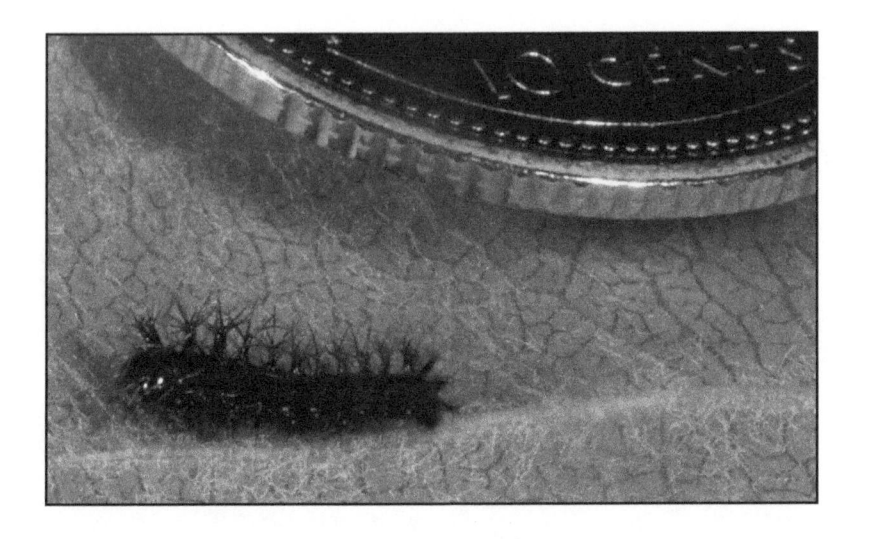

The newly hatched caterpillars or larvae are black and approximately the size of a mosquito.

The black spines quickly change to a light yellow. Young cecropias like to remain together until they become larger.

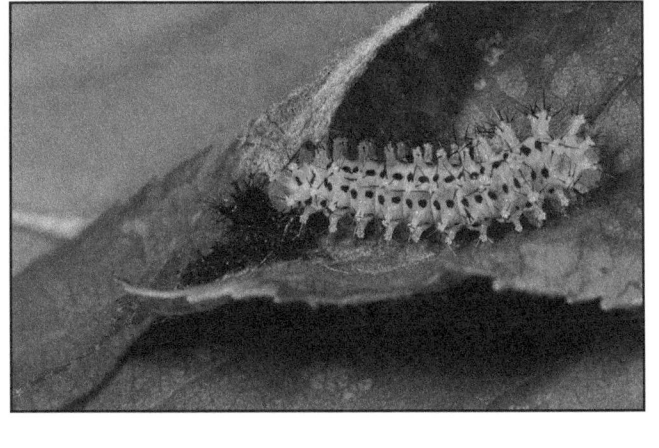

Silken pad   Second Instar molt

A cecropia caterpillar will eat a lot of leaves and get quite large. Its skin does not grow. When the caterpillar becomes so large that its skin becomes too tight, it will need new skin. It will have to molt or shed its old skin. The caterpillar will stop eating, and then it will spin silken pads and attach its hind legs to it. It will remain in a slightly curled position and not move for at least a day. There is a slight colour change when the new skin is ready to molt or shed.

Old skin

When the new skin is ready, the head skin will fall off and the moths will ripple and crawl forward so that the old skin moves back along their bodies until it forms a little bunch that is left behind on the silk pad. They will turn around and eat most, if not all, of the old skin before they move on to eat the leaves again.

A comparison of a Second, Third (2 of them) and Fourth Instar

These new caterpillar stages, or phases, are called instars. There are five stages. Notice the difference in the colour of each phase.

Instar phases

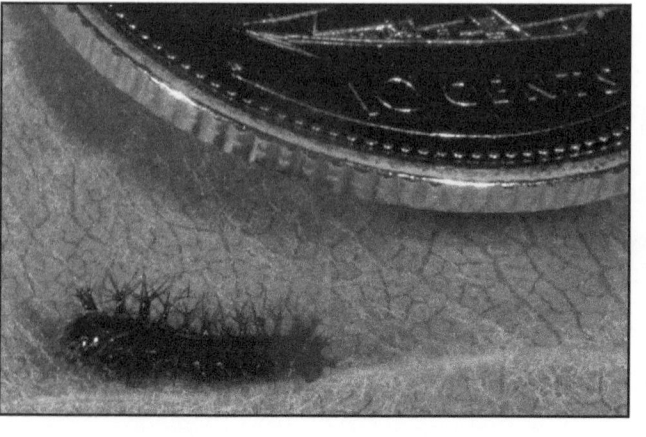

First Instar

Molt to Second Instar

Molt to Third Instar

Molt to Fourth Instar

The larvae will not move for nearly two days before shedding. The fifth instar is not quite as bright as the fourth, but it is very large in size! It now has blue "feet" on the prolegs.

Ready to spin a cocoon

Molt to fifth and
final instar.

It will eat day and night for about eight to ten days.

Upon reaching maturity in autumn, the moth is four to four and a half inches long. The caterpillar is now ready to spin a cocoon. It will not eat for about a day and then will become restless, crawling everywhere as it searches for the perfect place to spin its cocoon. Now it will purge, or empty its gut. It makes a cluster by attaching silk to everything it touches, usually pulling in several leaves and/or branches. The cecropia caterpillar will spend a few days spinning a tough, weather-resistant cocoon, leaving the top for last so that it can emerge easily in the spring. It will usually pupate for the winter.

The winters in Canada can be very cold, reaching temperatures of -30 to -40 degrees Celsius. The inside structure of the pupa is watertight. It manufactures large quantities of glycerol, a sugar alcohol, to use as antifreeze. Now it can spend the winter unaffected by temperatures that may plunge below -40 degrees Celsius. It will go through a metamorphosis in the coming spring.

Metamorphosis is a major change in the form or structure of some animals or insects that happens as the animal or insect becomes an adult.

The moth will emerge or push itself out as an adult moth in the first two weeks of seasonally warm weather in early summer. The cecropia moth has morphed, or changed, into an adult moth. It will emerge out of the top of the cocoon, usually in the middle of the day to allow it to warm up. This happens very quickly—in less than a minute!

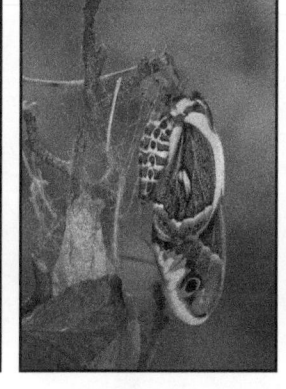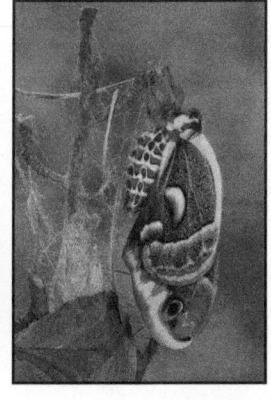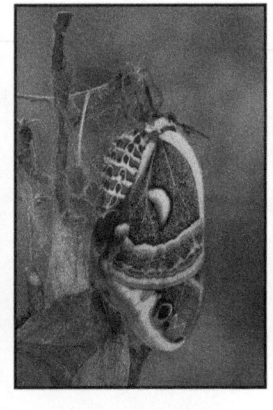

After the moth emerges from the top of the cocoon, blood flows from its thorax into the wings and then back into the thorax. The wings will grow much larger, or expand, as the moth spends the rest of the day pumping up and drying its wings. By the time it is dark, it can fly and look for a mate.

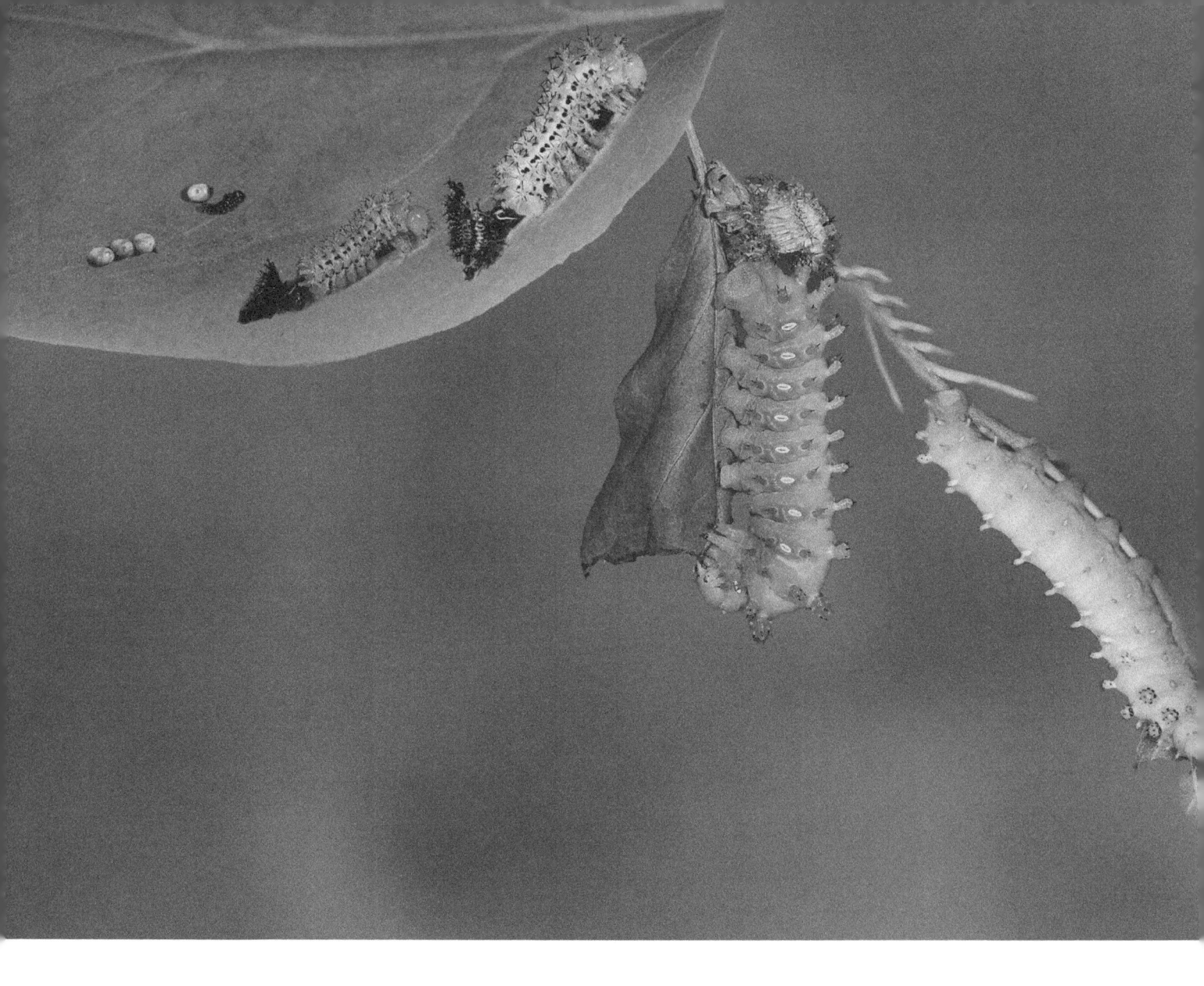

If by chance you ever see a cecropia
moth, remember the fascinating

transformation that took place
for it to become so beautiful.